Oceans

Clare Oliver
Consultant: Clive Carpenter

MiLes
KeLLy
PUBLISHING

First published in 2004 by
Miles Kelly Publishing Ltd
Bardfield Centre, Great Bardfield, Essex, CM7 4SL

Copyright © Miles Kelly Publishing Ltd 2004
2 4 6 8 10 9 7 5 3 1

Some material in this book can also be found in
100 Things You Should Know About Oceans

Editorial Director: Anne Marshall

Editors: Nicola Sail, Amanda Learmonth

Design: Maya Currell

British Library Cataloguing-in-Publication Data
A catalogue record for this book is available from the British Library

ISBN 1-84236-231-3

Printed in Singapore

ACKNOWLEDGEMENTS

The Publishers would like to thank the following artists
who have contributed to this book:

Kuo Kang Chen, Peter Dennis, Richard Draper, Nicholas Forder, Chris Forsey, Terry Gabbey,
Studio Galante, Alan Harris, Kevin Maddison, Alan Male, Janos Marffy, Steve Roberts,
Martin Sanders, Mike Saunders, Gwen Tourret, Rudi Vizi

Computer-generated cartoons by James Evans

www.mileskelly.net
info@mileskelly.net

Contents

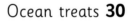

Water, water everywhere

Oceans cover over two-thirds of the Earth's rocky surface. Their total area is about 362 million square kilometres, which means there is more than twice as much ocean as land!

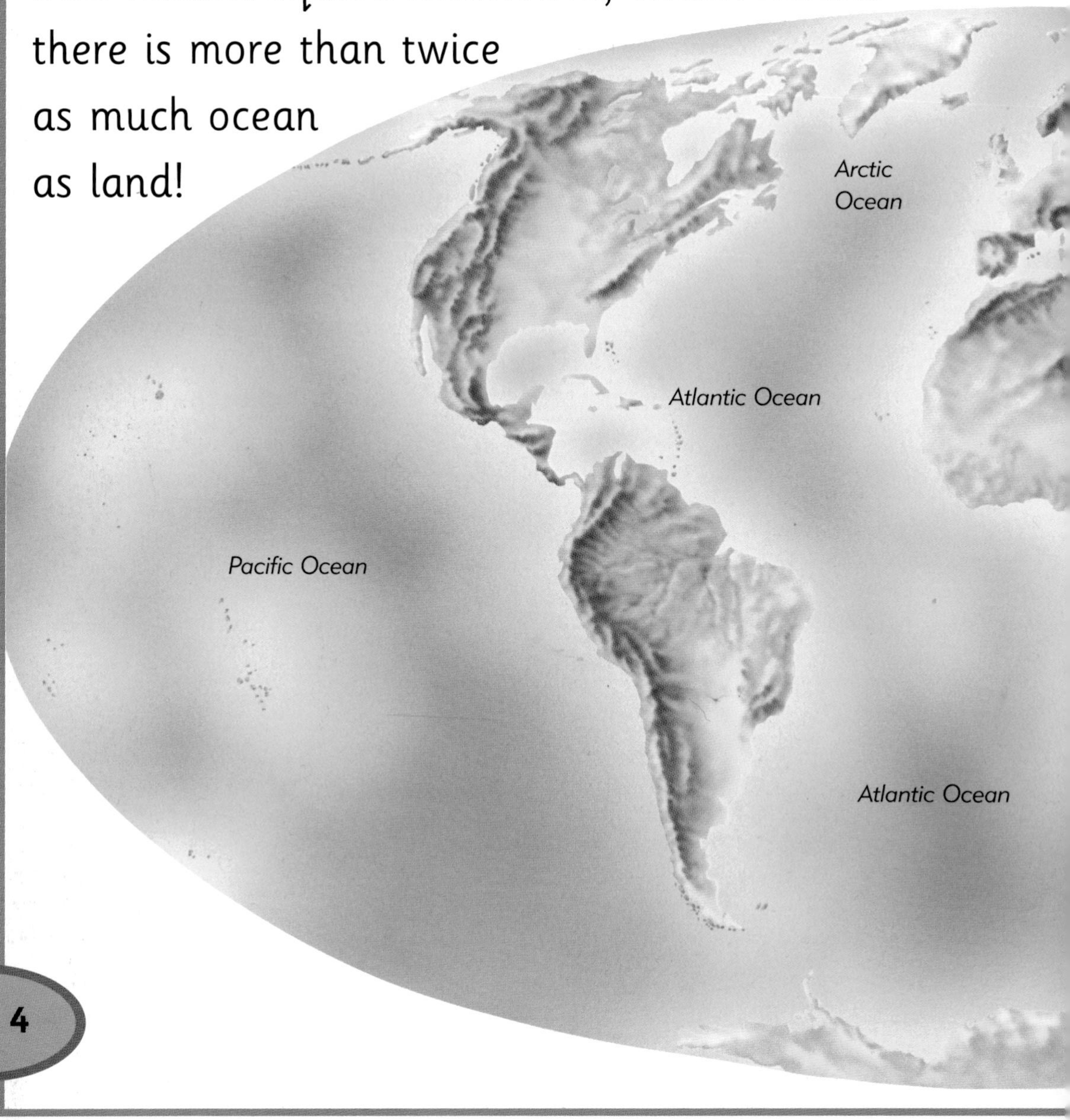

Arctic Ocean

Atlantic Ocean

Pacific Ocean

Atlantic Ocean

▼ Although all the oceans flow into each other, we know them as four different oceans – the Pacific, Atlantic, Indian and Arctic. Each ocean is made up of smaller bodies of water called seas.

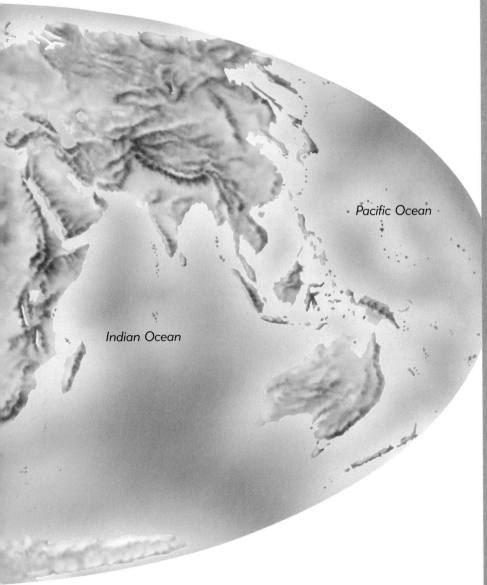

Pacific Ocean ·

Indian Ocean

In its deepest parts, the Pacific Ocean would cover the top of Mount Everest.

Waves on the surface of the ocean can carve into rocks creating shapes such as this sea stack.

Icebergs break off from huge glaciers and then drift and melt into the oceans.

Under the ocean

There are plains, mountains and valleys under the ocean, in areas called basins. Each basin has a rim (the flat continental shelf that meets the shore) and sides (the continental slope that drops away from the shelf). The ocean floor moves and its features are changing all the time.

▶ New islands are born all the time. When an underwater volcano erupts, its lava cools in the water. Layers of lava build up and the volcano grows in size until it peeps above the waves.

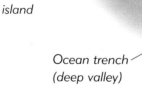

Volcanic island

Ocean trench (deep valley)

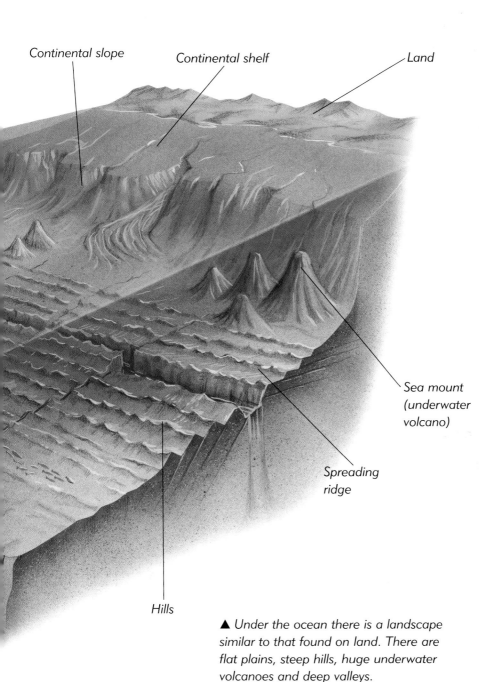

Continental slope

Continental shelf

Land

Sea mount
(underwater
volcano)

Spreading
ridge

Hills

▲ Under the ocean there is a landscape similar to that found on land. There are flat plains, steep hills, huge underwater volcanoes and deep valleys.

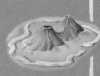

Stage 1
A coral reef may build up around a volcanic island.

Stage 2
The volcanic island sinks leaving a lagoon (water separate from the open ocean).

Stage 3
An atoll is the ring-shaped coral reef that is left behind and surrounds the lagoon.

7

Rock pool life

Rock pools are full of all kinds of creatures.
Limpets, sponges and anemones all attach
themselves to rocks, stopping the waves
washing them away. They eat scraps
of food washed in with the tide.
These pools are also the
perfect place for crabs
to find food and
to hide.

Limpets

Goby

Find the creature!

*Unscramble these words
to find the names of four
different sea creatures:*

1. PETLIM   *2.* NGEOPS

3. MONEENA   *4.* MITREH

1. LIMPET 2. SPONGE
3. ANEMONE 4. HERMIT

Starfish

8

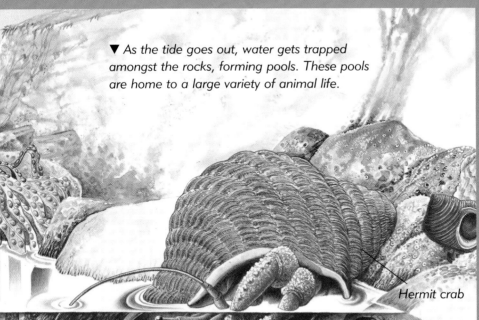

▼ As the tide goes out, water gets trapped amongst the rocks, forming pools. These pools are home to a large variety of animal life.

Hermit crab

Anemones are named after flowers, due to their arms that look like petals.

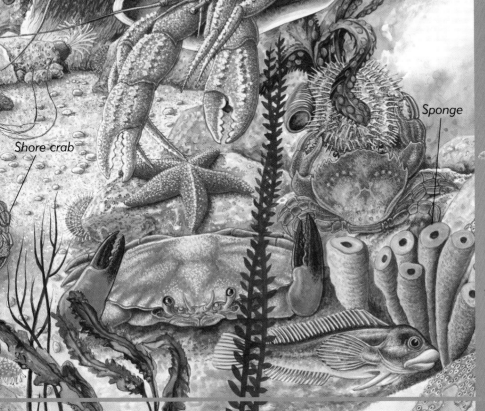

Sponge

Shore crab

Hermit crabs have no shell, so they use one left behind by another sea creature.

Starfish may lose one of their arms if attacked, but they can grow new ones.

9

Tropical life

Tiny animals build huge underwater walls.
The walls are built up from coral – the leftover
skeletons of sea creatures called polyps. Over
millions of years, enough skeletons pile up to form
huge, wall-like structures called reefs. Coral reefs
are full of all sorts of amazing,
colourful sea life.

Lion fish

Cleaner wrasse fish

Sea anemone

Stone fish

Test your memory!

1. In its deepest parts, which ocean would cover the top of Mount Everest?

2. Which animal uses a shell from another sea creature in which to live?

3. What is a ring-shaped coral reef called?

4. Name the world's four main oceans.

4. Pacific, Atlantic, Indian and Arctic
3. an atoll
1. Pacific Ocean 2. hermit crab

Cleaner wrasse fish nibble bits of dirt off bigger fishes' bodies.

Stone fish rest on the seabed and look exactly like stones!

Clownfish

Clownfish swim unharmed amongst sea anemones' tentacles.

▲ Most fish found in coral reefs have colourful spots or stripes. This helps them to blend with their surroundings, making it hard for a hunter to spot them.

Super swimmers

There are over 21,000 different types of fish in the sea. Almost all are covered in scales and use fins and a muscular tail to power themselves through the water. They have slits called gills that take oxygen from the water so that they can breathe.

Molly's fun facts!

Flying fish can use their winglike fins to keep them in the air for as long as 30 seconds!

Oarfish grow up to 8 metres long! Their length protects them from hunters.

Sunfish are so-called because they sunbathe on the ocean surface.

A flounder's shape and colour help to camouflage (hide) it on the seabed.

▲ In a large group called a school, fish like these yellow snappers have less chance of being caught by hunters.

Awesome jaws!

Sharks don't have bones. Their skeletons are made of a gristly substance called cartilage. All sharks are meat-eaters. Some filter tiny prey from the water, or lie in wait for victims on the seabed. Others speed through the ocean after prey.

▲ *Great white sharks can speed through the water at 30 kilometres an hour.*

Test your memory!

1. What length might an oarfish reach?
2. What type of animal is a limpet?
3. What are coral reefs built up from?

3. skeletons of sea creatures called polyps
1. up to 8 metres 2. a shellfish

Basking sharks eat huge amounts of tiny sea creatures called plankton.

▼ The blue shark can be dangerous and is known to attack humans.

Dorsal fin

Ampullae of Lorenzini (to sense electricity from nearby fish)

Nostril

Jaw

Pectoral fin

Tail fin

Anal fin

Pelvic fin

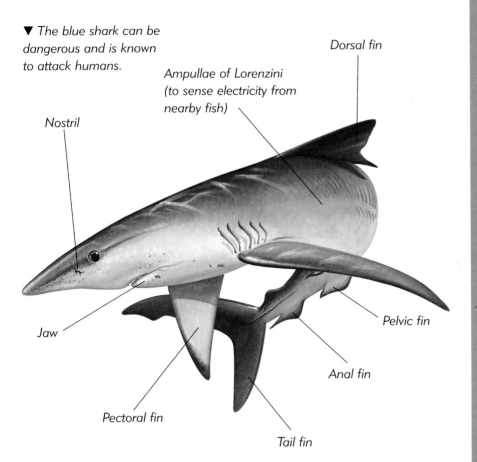

Hammerhead sharks have a nostril and an eye on each end of their hammer-shaped head.

Tiger sharks may produce as many as 40 babies.

15

Sea mammals

Whales have to come to the surface for air. This is because they are mammals, like we are. Sperm whales hold their breath for the longest period of time – up to two hours. Some whales have sievelike parts in their mouth called baleen, for filtering food through.

Baleen

▼ The blue whale is the biggest animal on the planet. It measures about 28 metres in length!

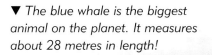

When a sperm whale surfaces it blows stale air from its blowhole.

The beluga whale is also known as the 'sea canary' because of the sweet song it uses to communicate.

Blue whale young are called calves. They feed on their mother's rich milk until they are about eight months old

Molly's fun facts!

Barnacles are shellfish. They attach themselves to ships' hulls, or the bodies of grey whales and other large sea animals.

Fast flippers

Seals, sea lions and walruses are warm-blooded mammals that have adapted to ocean life. These creatures are known as pinnipeds, meaning 'fin feet'. They have flippers instead of legs and a streamlined body. Instead of fur, they have a layer of fat called blubber to keep them warm in chilly waters.

Sea otters live off the Pacific coast among huge forests of seaweed called kelp.

Walruses use their tusks to break breathing holes in the ice and to pull themselves out of the water.

▲ The male southern elephant seal is as big as a real elephant. It is almost 6 metres long and weighs about 5 tonnes!

Molly's fun facts!

Leopard seals sing in their sleep! These seals, found in the Antarctic, chirp and whistle while they snooze.

Cold-blooded creatures

▶▲ *When marine iguanas are not diving for food, they bask on the rocks that dot the island coastlines. The lizards' dark skin helps to absorb (take in) the Sun's heat.*

Cold-blooded creatures, such as reptiles, cannot control their body temperature like we can. This is why they prefer life on land, where it is easier for them to warm up. But there are some reptiles that have adapted to ocean life.

◀ *Banded sea snakes swim around coral reefs in search of their favourite food – eels.*

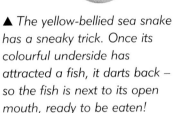

Marine iguanas *live on the Galapagos Islands in the Pacific Ocean.*

▲ *The yellow-bellied sea snake has a sneaky trick. Once its colourful underside has attracted a fish, it darts back – so the fish is next to its open mouth, ready to be eaten!*

Banded sea snakes *use venom (poison) to stun prey.*

Mix and match

Can you match these sea turtles to their names?

1. Green **2.** Hawksbill
3. Leatherback
4. Loggerhead

a.

b.

c.

d.

1. c 2. b 3. d 4. a

▲ *Leatherbacks are the biggest turtles in the world and can grow up to 4 metres in length.*

A sea snake's venom *is more poisonous than that of any land snake.*

21

Deep sea creatures

Few creatures can survive in the dark, icy-cold ocean depths. Food is so hard to find that creatures living there have very unusual features to help them survive. In the icy depths you will find glow-in-the-dark fish, fish with invisible teeth and even fish with their own fishing rods!

◀ Black swallowers are just 25 centimetres long but can eat fish far bigger than themselves. Their loose jaws unhinge to fit over their prey and their body stretches to take in their huge meal.

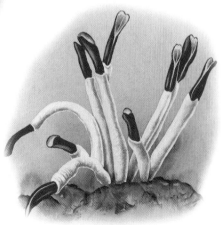

▶ Giant tubeworms grow around hot spots on the ocean floor. They feed on tiny particles that they collect from the water.

Test your memory!

1. Which is the biggest animal on Earth?

2. How long might an elephant seal be?

3. Which is the biggest turtle in the world?

4. Where do marine iguanas live?

1. the blue whale 2. almost 6 metres long 3. the leatherback turtle 4. on the Galapagos Islands in the Pacific Ocean

Cookiecutters take biscuit-shaped bites out of their prey's body!

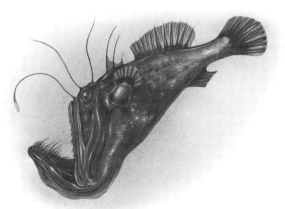

◄ The anglerfish has a stringy 'fishing rod' with a glowing tip that hangs above its jaw. This attracts small fish to its mouth, which it then catches and eats.

Dragon fish have light organs dotted along their sides and belly to tempt prey and confuse hunters.

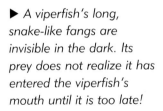

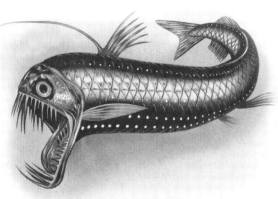

▶ A viperfish's long, snake-like fangs are invisible in the dark. Its prey does not realize it has entered the viperfish's mouth until it is too late!

Lantern fish have bodies that glow.

23

Great travellers

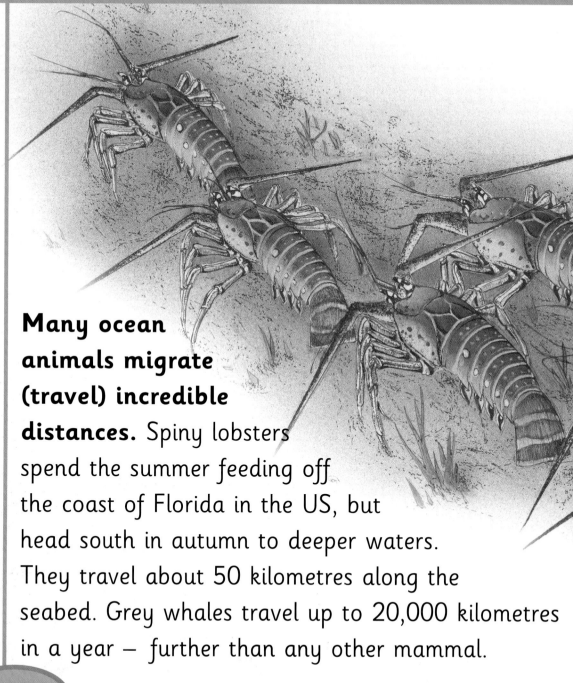

Many ocean animals migrate (travel) incredible distances. Spiny lobsters spend the summer feeding off the coast of Florida in the US, but head south in autumn to deeper waters. They travel about 50 kilometres along the seabed. Grey whales travel up to 20,000 kilometres in a year – further than any other mammal.

▶ Grey whales travel south in winter to the warmer waters of Mexico, where they have their babies. In summer they swim back to the food-rich waters off the coast of Alaska.

Alaska

Mexico

Loggerhead turtle babies make a two-year journey from the beaches in Japan to Mexico.

An Arctic tern can fly more than 40,000 kilometres in one year!

▲ Spiny lobsters travel in columns that may be more than 50-strong. They keep together by touch, using their long, spiky antennae (feelers).

Molly's fun facts!

Eels and salmon swim thousands of kilometres from the sea to spawn (lay eggs) in the same place where they were born.

Air aces

Wandering albatross

Wandering albatrosses are the biggest sea birds. With a wingspan of around three metres, these sea birds are so large they take off by launching from a cliff. They are such expert gliders that they even sleep whilst flying. All kinds of birds live near the oceans – birds with coloured bills, bright red pouches and colourful feet.

▶ Many birds make nests on a high cliff ledge. Puffins often scrape their own burrows, or they may take over an abandoned rabbit hole.

Gannets can dive into water from a height of 30 metres.

Male frigate birds puff up their bright red pouch to show off to females.

Boobies dance to show off their red or blue feet.

Identify the sea bird!

See if you can match these sea birds to their correct names:

Grey headed gull   Cormorant   Black tern

a.   **b.**   **c.**

a. black tern b. grey headed gull c. cormorant

All kinds of penguin

Gentoo penguin

Chinstrap penguin

Adélie penguin

There are 17 different types of penguin and most live around the Antarctic. They feed on fish, squid and krill. Their black-and-white plumage is important camouflage. Seen from above, a penguin's black back blends in with the water.
  Seen from underneath, the white belly is difficult to see against the sunlit surface of the sea.

King penguin

Emperor penguin

An Adélie penguin builds its nest from stones and small rocks.

The emperor penguin chick is kept warm in its father's belly feathers.

▲ Penguins can swim, but not fly. They have oily, waterproofed feathers and flipper-like wings. Instead of lightweight, hollow bones – like a flying bird's – some penguins have solid heavy bones. This helps them to stay underwater longer when diving for food.

Molly's fun facts!

The fastest swimming bird is the gentoo penguin. It has been known to swim at speeds of 27 kilometres an hour!

Ocean treats

Oceans give us many delicious things to eat. Some farmers grow seaweed that can be eaten on its own and is also a useful ingredient in products such as ice cream. Fishermen gather oysters from the seabed – and catch lobsters in pots!

▲ In shallow, tropical waters, some farmers grow their own seaweed in plots on the seabed.

Test your memory!

1. What is the wingspan of an albatross?

2. How far do spiny lobsters travel along the seabed?

3. What is the fastest swimming penguin?

4. How far might an Arctic tern fly in one year?

3. gentoo penguin 4. more than 40,000 kilometres

1. about three metres 2. about 50 kilometres

Harvested seaweed is dried in the sun to preserve it.

▶ Pearls are precious gems made by oysters. If a grain of sand gets inside and irritates its soft body, the oyster coats the sand with a substance called nacre. Over many years, the nacre builds up and the pearl becomes larger.

Oysters are one of the most popular foods taken from the sea.

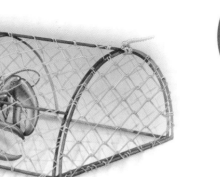

Adult lobsters are caught in pots filled with fish bait.

▲ Fishermen attach buoys (brightly-coloured floating objects) to their lobster pots, so they can remember where to find them again.

31

The high seas

Pirates once ruled the high seas. Pirates are sailors who attack and board other ships to steal their cargoes. Their golden age was during the 1600s and 1700s. This was when ships carried treasures, weapons and goods back to Europe from the Americas, Africa and Asia.

▶ Piracy was a man's world but some women pirates also took to the high seas. Two women, Mary Read and Anne Bonny, were part of a crew that sailed around the Caribbean.

▶ The bed of the Caribbean Sea is scattered with the remains of Spanish galleons, many of which still hold treasure.

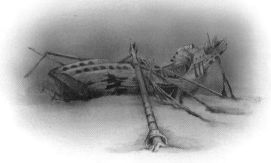

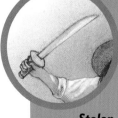

Stolen weapons were used by pirates on raids.

Rigging was often used to climb up and adjust the sails.

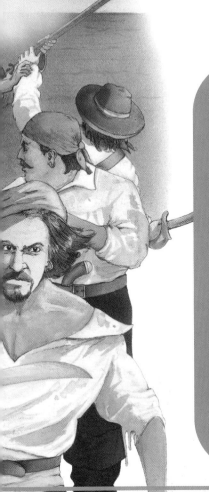

Pirate flag!

You will need:
- paper • paints
- brushes

The skull-and-crossbones is the most famous pirate flag, but it was not the only one. Use your paints and brushes to copy one of these designs!

Women pirates wore men's clothes and used fighting weapons, such as daggers.

33

Travelling underwater

The first submarine made its test dive in 1776 – and could only carry one person! Submarines have improved since then, becoming bigger and faster. The biggest were Russian submarines called *Typhoons,* which were built in the 1970s and 1980s.

Living quarters

▶ Typhoon *submarines weighed 26,500 tonnes and travelled the fastest – reaching speeds of up to 40 knots.*

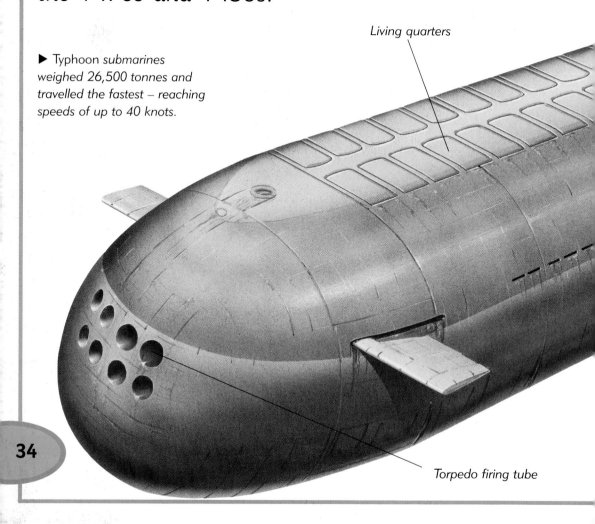

Torpedo firing tube

Periscope

Engine room

Divers wear cylinders of gas, including oxygen, on their back so they can breathe underwater.

The Turtle was the first submarine – it could only hold one person.

The Trieste submarine travelled to the deepest part of the Pacific Ocean.

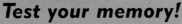

Test your memory!

1. What precious gems are made by oysters?

2. What cold food might seaweed be used in?

3. Which two women pirates sailed with a crew around the Caribbean?

1. pearls 2. ice cream 3. Mary Read and Anne Bonny

Water fun

The first sea sport was surfing. It became popular in the 1950s, but was invented centuries earlier in Hawaii. Waimea Bay in Hawaii is one of the best places to surf – surfers catch waves that are up to 11 metres high! Today, there are many sea sports that people take part in, both professionally and just for fun.

▶ Modern surfboards are made of super-light materials. This means that surfers can reach high speeds.

Hydroplanes are motor boats that skim across the surface of the water.

▶ Jet skis were developed in the 1960s. Their inventor was called Clayton Jacobsen. He wanted to combine his two favourite hobbies – motorbikes and waterskiing.

hull

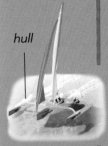

Trimarans have three hulls that cut through the water.

Word scramble

Unscramble these words to find the names of four different sea sports:

1. GNIFSUR   **2.** LINGSAI

3. TEJ-KISING **4.** TERSKIWAING

1. SURFING 2. SAILING 3. JET-SKIING 4. WATERSKIING

Waterskiing is now one of the most popular watersports.

37

Ocean tales

The ancient Greeks made up lots of sea adventure stories, probably because they lived on scattered islands. In the legend of the Argonauts, a hero called Jason sets off in a boat called the *Argos* with a band of brave men. He goes on a quest to find the Golden Fleece, a precious sheepskin guarded by a fierce dragon.

▼ Jason and the Argonauts steer their ship between two huge moving cliffs called the Cyanean Rocks. They faced many dangers on their journey.

Aphrodite, the beautiful Greek goddess, is said to have been born in the sea.

The giant squid may have inspired tales of a giant sea monster, called the kraken.

Molly's fun facts!

A mermaid's purse is the name given to the eggcases of the dog shark. They look a bit like handbags!

Index